Amsterdam. Paved into its streets is an artistic heritage centuries old. And though its liberal laws and relaxed environment have pulled in tourists in recent decades, the city offers much more than canals and coffee shops.

The legacy of the Dutch Masters lives on, transformed, in a new generation of innovative artists and designers. The docks and wharfs of the Noord are examples of abandoned corners that have been reclaimed and reinvigorated. Even the architecture has been reinterpreted, with a modern spin on the classic canal house.

But for LOST iN it's the people who shape the city's atmosphere. For this new Amsterdam issue we spoke with talents from various fields: a fashion designer, an artist couple, a film creative, a DJ and a chef. Get lost in the city of transformation. Get lost in Amsterdam.

The Marineterrein on an island behind Amsterdam's Central Station was originally built in the 17th century to house the Dutch Navy, but has seen an impressive rebuilding project. Architecture buffs are often found gathered in front of Marine Base Amsterdam Building 27E, a former naval training centre transformed by one of the country's most renowned architects, Bureau SLA. The Bureau souped it up considerably for the 2016 Dutch presidency of the Council of the European Union,

with geometric window screens inspired by the flags of EU member nations. Other wild Marineterrein incarnations include Pension Homeland, an officers' residence renovated into a Mad Men-style hotel. In keeping with the theme, famed waterside dining spot Scheepskameel is based in the former naval kitchen.

• Marineterrein Amsterdam, Kattenburgerstraat 5, Centrum

Culture | Die Happy

Once a morgue and anatomical laboratory, now the only things being dissected here are movie narratives. *Lab 111* offers up a host of film-related exhibitions and a roster of cult classics, short arthouse pieces and in-depth documentaries that can be enjoyed with or without dinner in the adjacent Strangelove restaurant—named after Stanley Kubrick's classic. Dead interesting for popcorn munching blockbuster lovers as well as chin stroking cinephiles.

• Lab 111, West, lab111.nl

From Space Age Furniture to Pine Ice Cream

High Density

Food | Swine and Dine

The restaurant *Wilde Zwijnen* (pictured) was a trendsetter for "New Dutch Cuisine", spawning many imitators, but few can match its pared-down cuisine made from locally sourced produce. The Boar's next-door sister was born in 2015—*Bar Bachrach* provides creative tapas in a more casual and late-night setting. Meanwhile, another foody treasure of the Oost is rustic French kitchen *La Vallade*. Set along a dijk, it feels like the home of a hospitable aunt with an open cellar. The restaurant's set menu and fantastic house wine will hardly break a 50 euro note.

• Various locations, Oost

Culture **Image Conscious**

Before the days of www, when Narda van 't Veer was running a successful creative agency, a collection of photography started that continues to this day—in the form of *The Ravestijn Gallery* (pictured), founded along with Jasper Bode. The gallery respresents some of the country's most respected photographers, including Blommers & Schumm and Inez & Vindoodh. The curatorial duo have an eye for style; from esoteric and erotica to fashion, the place drips photographic erudition.

Annet Gelink is another juicy stop on the city's art trail, wedged between the Nine Streets and narrow bridges of the Jordaan. Here, highbrow groundbreaking work meets young, up-and-coming practitioners in a serene space that encourages you to invest in what you are seeing.

• The Ravestijn Gallery, West, theravestijngallery.com;
Annet Gelink, Centrum, annetgelink.com

Food

Airwaves to Appetizers

In 1964, a rogue broadcasting platform in the North Sea dared to challenge the Dutch airwaves with pirate radio and television. Three months later, a government raid silenced the signal, but not its legacy. Reborn in 2011, the steel platform made its return, not as a broadcaster, but as a culinary destination. Now perched on stilts in the Nieuwe Houthaven harbor, *REM Eiland* offers a unique three-tiered experience: The first floor houses a stylish bar, the second a dining area, and a panoramic lounge crowns the rooftop with sweeping views of the river and skyline. The restaurant showcases refined European cuisine, featuring both à la carte selections and a tasting menu, all served in an industrial chic setting that honors its rebel roots.

• REM, Haparandadam 45, Houthaven, rem.amsterdam

Shop

Dress to the Nines

The Nine Streets (Negen Straatjes) unfolds as a treasure trove of boutiques, galleries, vintage finds and 17th-century architecture in the heart of the canal ring. This enclave—a grid of three parallel streets across four principal canals—reveals a wealth of artisan shops at every turn. Redefine rainy-day fashion at *Rainkiss* with colorful ponchos crafted from recycled plastic bottles, or journey through the sartorial styles of the fifties to eighties at *Zipper*, or indulge in fondue and 400 varieties of cheese at *De Kaaskamer.* A short stroll north leads to *MICKKEUS* (pictured), a denim atelier with bespoke tailoring that turns vintage Levi's 501s into unique expressions of personal style.

• Various, Negen Straatjes in de Jordaan

Shop · Mad Finds

Having first begun in 1985 along the now quaint shopping street of Utrechtsestraat, interior connoisseurs Dick Dankers and Cok de Rooy slowly built up a collection from big brands and undiscovered creatives side by side, featuring everything from wallpaper to heating elements to pimp up your home or office. Stock at their store *Frozen Fountain* (pictured) ranges from small pieces for ten euros you could take home, to designer sofas worth ten grand that you might just wistfully gaze at. Open one long weekend per month in Zeeburgerpad, *Fortune Flea* offers vintage finds from all over France and Belgium. Find pottery, furniture and fabrics no longer in production, but set to outlast any trend.
• Frozen Fountain, Centrum, frozenfountain.nl; Fortune Flea, Oost, fortuneflea.com

Food · Western Delights

The West sparkles with sophisticated sustenance options. Named after a street where the restaurant owners met and partied, *Binnenvisser* (pictured) provides a menu way more seasonal and farm-derived than the fare they were probably having back then. There are the ubiquitous tasting plates of vegetable-focussed dishes, with a fine selection of natural wines. Up on the third floor of warehouse-turned-theatre Het Veem, overlooking the IJ river, is *Bak*. Originally a pop-up operating in empty spaces across the city, it laid roots here. Its changing menu of ethically sourced dishes includes well thought-out combinations like roe deer stew and bone marrow terrine with charred kale, or celeriac with pine ice cream for dessert.
• Various locations, West

David Laport
He started out in costume design before embarking on a career collaborating with the Dutch National Ballet and freelancing for global brands, and later establishing his own eponymous brand. His appreciation of a distinctive silhouette has led him to design couture pieces for the world's most empowered female artists including Solange, Sia and Rihanna

David Laport, Fashion Designer

Open Minded

From his office in a 17th century canal house, part of a UNESCO World Heritage Site, Laport talks cinema, Amsterdam fashion, and the spots he visits to let off steam

The Movies
Centrum

FilmHallen
West

Kriterion
Centrum

Libertine Petit Café
Centrum

Homeland Brewery
Centrum

Pllek
Noord

Noorderlicht
Noord

Sexyland
Noord

Tolhuistuin
Noord

Garage Noord
Noord

Café de Tuin
Centrum

So, you worked in a cinema for some time, tell us about it.

Well, I am obsessed with the cinema. I know that we have more film houses per capita than any other European city. From disused tram service stations to the more commercial larger ones. They all have their own quirks. *The Movies* where I used to work, is the oldest functioning cinema in the city. The *FilmHallen* is great too and of course the *Kriterion*, an art-house movie theater founded by anti-Nazi students in 1945. It still has that student vibe too.

Describe your ideal Amsterdam day.

On weekends I try to stay off my bike and do things at my own pace. I will wake up and head down Haarlemmerstraat for a coffee and then go to the Noordermarkt to buy some flowers and groceries. That market has the best energy around 11am on a Saturday. I go over the bridge where the Brouwersgracht meets the sun and I can already feel the buzz. I then will most likely bump into a friend, so we will have a coffee at *Libertine* and then I might wander the Nine Streets before heading to the studio for a couple of hours. Then I will head down to Utrechtsestraat, another shopping street I love, and meet with friends who live down there too. Summer days are a little different, the city really blossoms. I would move to the Marineterrein Amsterdam and Homeland Brewery is the place to be, as you can swim there! If I were to head Noord then I would meet friends at *Pllek* or the *Noorderlicht*.

Where do you like to party?

So, my friends are the ones that really help me with this. I rely on them to find me the parties to go to, and they never disappoint. We sometimes end up at an underground party in Sloterdijk. In the Noord we would head to *Sexyland* or even the *Tolhuistuin* for laidback drinks. *Garage Noord* is also great and super underground. If you have an open mind, you are sure to have a good time in any of these places. Amsterdam also has a few great bars around the centre like *Café De Tuin*.

Why haven't you moved to one of the "fashion" capitals yet?

Amsterdam is very international. Yet it is super low key. It is big and small as a city, all at the same time. We have a standard of living that would be difficult to match in cities like New York or London. The cost of living, the effort of transport and also the spread of the city is a lot to deal with, which changes your day to day lifestyle by a lot. I love Paris and it would be suited to what I do, but again, it is so big and busy, I just don't know whether or not I would enjoy living there as much. Here, I can do everything in one day. From the Oost to the Centre, to swimming in the Noord and then back home. In Amsterdam, nothing is too much of an effort.

How would you describe Amsterdam fashion?

We are a jeans country. We love denim and we wear it many different ways. Our style is relaxed, but there is always a classic edge to what we do. Women dress up but may wear some chic flats. The Amsterdam woman is a little rock and roll. Even if people have money, they don't want to wear it. My sequinned trousers are best sellers, and out of everything I would say they are the most relaxed piece I have designed.

FilmHallen is one of the varied cinemas making Amsterdam a cinephile capital

The Duchess
Centrum

Conservatorium Hotel
Zuid

Cecconi's
Centrum

Mata Hari
Centrum

Timboektoe
Wijk aan Zee

De Cuevel
Noord

Baut
Various locations

If you wanted to dress up, where would you go?

I am not really a dinner person, but I do know where people go when they want to dress for an occasion. I would suggest *The Duchess* or the *Conservatorium Hotel*, which I have recently done some work with. *Cecconi's*, which is part of Soho House, is also nice with live jazz and relaxed food. There is also a bar and restaurant in the Red Light District, which is a piece of history in a way. It's called *Mata Hari*, named after the Dutch exotic dancer and even though it's in the middle of the city's busiest part, it's a retreat from the chaos.

You are a real lover of nature, tell us where you go?

It doesn't take much to find nature in this city. The north is super beautiful and hardly any effort to get to, but it feels miles away. Wijk aan Zee is a great beach with a bar called *Timboektoe*, which is always fun. You can bike or take the scooter to Durgerdammerdijk and end up at *De Ceuvel* in the north, which serves local and organic food. In the summer you can swim there if you dare.

What tips do you have for people visiting the city?

There is a company called Barqo, which is basically like Airbnb but for boats. People will take you out on their boat, you have a captain and you can see the 1680 bridges of this city without having to worry about how to get back. Another place I really like is *Baut*, which used to be a travelling restaurant that you would have to look up to find. It has great food.

Noord

Over the Pond

Once known for crime and containers the North's grit is now sprinkled among TV stations, markets, luxe kitchens and party spots. Take the North-South metro or the free ferry across the water to this fresh shore

Night | **Don't Stop the Dance**

Probably start with a quiet drink in the bohemian greenhouse vibe of the *Noorderlicht Café*, with a band playing in the amphitheatre. To turn the music up and the dance on, *Veronicaschip* was once used by radio station Veronica to transmit shows, and now provides drinks and private events. If being on board doesn't float your boat, *Sexyland* lies just across the road. Here, each night offers a different host the right to do what they please with the place, from sporting events to gangsta rap nights. *Garage Noord* recalls the now-shuttered De School in West Amsterdam, but for those across the water. With a good menu of healthy portions, you can eat here, then dance til 5am. Holding around 150 people, the small venue was first started by the people behind Red Light Records. Now, lovers of anything underground come by for dirty electro, reggae or punk, without any inner city aggression. Most of the venues in Noord have the impending threat of being torn down due new constructions, so these people know how to live each day like it's the last.
• Various locations, Noord

Culture · Food **Primary Living**

An arthouse movie cinema with chairs eschewing numerical order. A petit restaurant serving an ever-changing menu of dishes made in a wood-fired oven. A collection of natural wines and ciders. *FC Hyena* is the living room we always wanted. Decorated in primary colours, because the paint was discounted, the resulting green flooring, blue bathrooms and red typeface come together in the most serendipitous way—rather in keeping with all things Noord. Showing a combo of arthouse and mainstream cinema, FC Hyena screens anything worthy of an audience.
• FC Hyena, Aambeeldstraat 24, fchyena.nl

Food **Ramping Up**

Despite being so busy they asked us not to include them in these pages, *Skatecafe* manages to stay as laid back as you can get without being fully reclined. A concrete mini and micro ramp greets you on (free) entry, the staff are relaxed and the food is good—get the grilled cheese sandwich if it's on offer. When you come to Noord you want a place to relax in, where food is easy and drinks within arm's reach. You have all this here with some beats to bounce to as well. They even welcome kids.
• Skatecafe, Gedempt Hamerkanaal 42, skatecafe.nl

Shop **Get the Goods**

What first began as a stall on the Noordermarkt has morphed into a warehouse just outside of the city of more than 2,500m² in size, and become the place to find home or garden furniture pieces with a story to tell. Weekly drops of vintage, antique furniture and fittings of every kind are at *Van Dijk & Ko*, categorised for easy discovery by the browsing eye. From French Belle Époque to New Scandinavian Design, there is something for every taste or need, from pottery and jars to front doors and Dutch books.
• Van Dijk & Ko, Pieter Ghijsenlaan 12A, Zaandam, vandijkenko.nl

Food **Food Bank**

The people from Hotel De Goudfazant were determined to feed more mouths in Amsterdam, and so opened a second eatery in the shape of *Café Modern*. Located in a former bank, pared-back furniture meets with the old-world style of this once commercial building. Even the bathrooms pay tribute, set into the bank's former safe. As with many good Amsterdam restaurants Café Modern offers a table d'hôte of four-courses with seasonal ingredients.

• Café Modern, Meidoornweg 2, modernamsterdam.nl

Culture **Kinetic Kino**

An imposing modernist structure from the outside makes way for a cinematic welcome. Divided into exhibition space, eatery, viewing deck and cinema, the *EYE Filmmuseum* offers a permanent exhibit regarding the history of the silver screen —with quiz booths to test every film buff. Classic flicks can be seen in four large cinemas while three smaller screening rooms rotate arthouse titles. Travelling exhibits have ranged from a collection of Stanley Kubrick film artifacts to a virtual reality experience from performance artist Marina Abramovic.

• EYE Filmmuseum, IJpromenade 1, eyefilm.nl

Food **Grass Fed**

Graze on organic, all-corn tacos from early evening to late night at *Coba*. The small team of chefs and waitstaff enforce quality here, with a weekly changing menu of seasonal dishes, littered with vegetarian and vegan options. The tacos, quesadillas and home-made salsas will help either your pre- or post-drink needs—or mid-drink if you opt for mescal or a cocktail garnished with a crunchy grasshopper. Big groups are rarely accomodated, preserving the intimate feeling of this plant-filled, colour-accented space.

• Coba Taqueria, Noord, coba-taqueria.com

Culture | Off the Grid

Don't let the websites deceive you, these galleries are quite legitimate. With one compared to London's White Cube and the other outlandishly contemporary and based in a former pharmacy, these new-world spaces are light years (or a North-South line) away from those found in Museumplein. The former, *Het HEM* (pictured), was founded by the guys behind the city's original sneaker paradise Patta. Their initiative is a favourite of Fantastic Man magazine's Gert Jonkers, who encourages people to visit. Het HEM is a place of artistic respite, forcing you to see a different side of Amsterdam —both metaphorically and literally. Hiding in plain sight in quiet suburbia, *De Apotheek* houses art shows with a little edge. With past exhibitions named "Tupac and Biggie" or "Buffer Zone," you should get an idea. Visit this temporary gallery while it lasts—with a nonchalant vibe in its pharmaceutical setting, it welcomes anyone who considers contemporary art worth digging around for. Like a good chat to a stranger on a bus, or accidentally ending up at a vernissage during a wild night out, these two spaces offer something you didn't know you needed, but very much want. As art should be.

• Various locations

Iwan Driessen

A trained chef in Japanese, Italian and French cuisine, Driessen is one of three chefs behind the famed Amsterdam restaurant Rijsel and its cousin Scheepskameel, which have been crowded with diners, night after night, for almost a decade

Iwan Driessen, Chef

Back to Basics

An Amsterdammer through and through, Driessen lives in the Nieuwmarkt area with his Japanese wife and family. With over 30 years of experience and a forte in good terrine, French sauces and sausage making, he reveals here the essence of the Dutch kitchen

Patisserie Holtkamp
Centrum

Brandt & Levie
Westpoort

RIJKS
Zuid

Fromagerie
Abraham Kef
Various locations

You were raised in Amsterdam, how have you seen the food industry change since you were a kid?

Before the war, the Dutch were a little more daring with what they ate. We had offal and beef tongue. We appreciated good cuts of meat and knew how to pair them with vegetables to get the best from a handful of flavours. It isn't unlike how I run my kitchen now. Good veal stock, salt, pepper and butter with some red wine and shallots can make a good sauce if you do it right. It's a lot harder to make simple food taste good because one mistake will be very obvious.

So, what happened with the way Dutch people ate, after the war?

We were limited with what we could get in terms of produce. Stamppot, a mashed potato and sausage-based meal, became standard. The building that houses Rijsel used to be a school where girls learned to be good housewives, for the want of a better description. This type of school was common after the war: girls learned to sew, make simple food and do the best with what they had.

Simple food is key to a Dutch kitchen, right?

It is, but it is also difficult to produce. When you think of masters in their field, *Patisserie Holtkamp* is exceptional. *Brandt & Levie* make very good cured sausages and have helped the younger generation become more knowledgeable regarding the quality of products and sustainability. Their food movement is linked to the Slow Food association, which has saved the food industry in a way. Joris Bijdendijk from the *RIJKS* restaurant has made an outstanding effort to educate people on food. He put goat on the menu and has worked with a poultry farmer to raise Anjou pigeons. That's helping the industry from the ground up. I am also very fond of *Fromagerie Abraham Kef*, a cheese shop in Oost whose owners have a great nose for new cheeses. They recently found a blue cheese made from buffalo milk which is a real eye opener. There are those making the effort to bring these things back.

Tell us about your time at Le Hollandais.

I learned equal amounts from two kitchens: Le Hollandais and a Japanese restaurant in Centrum. But in terms of taste it was Le Hollandais that set me on my path. I learned how sauces are built up and the function of the salt/sour balance, which is a skill in itself. It broadens and gives depth to a sauce and it also helps the sommelier. There, I realised that having a very good relationship with the serving staff is not to be underestimated. These people are the ones taking the dish to the table. They need to understand the meal as well as you have made it. What I adopted from my time at Le Hollandais is that being relaxed and not making concessions on quality is paramount. It is up there with not being an asshole to staff.

Can you define an Amsterdam dining experience?

We are a modest people. We are a Calvinist society. You know, years ago a typical waiter would be drinking a coffee with the other waiters at the bar. They would look at an entering customer like they were interrupting them. They had other jobs and waiting wasn't their lifelong ambition. I wanted to take the Parisian service standard and bring it to the restaurant here. The Bouillon Chartier in Paris has waiters that won't let you lift your

The wine pairs with the food as well as the canal view at Gebr. Hartering

Gebr. Hartering
Centrum

Hortus Botanicus
Centrum

Dappermarkt
Oost

Hotel De Goudfazant
Noord

't Loosje
Centrum

De Hapjeshoek
Centrum

head without checking that you are okay. These men are up to 60 years old. They have lived to wait tables. It's important that every aspect of the dining experience is carried out by someone who is passionate about it.

When you dine out, where do you go?

Gebr. Hartering (the Brothers Hartering) really has something special. The wine pairings they do as a duo are effortless. I recently went with a friend who ordered the most expensive white wine on the menu. Along with the traditional set menu, I also ordered a Brussel sprout dish, served with home-made oyster sauce and almonds. I have to say the wine merged with the dish perfectly. You need to understand flavours on a different level to get it this right.

Describe a perfect day in Amsterdam.

This is a quiet town, but with a very international feel, so try to explore all the different areas if you can. I would start with the Monday morning market at Noordermarkt, then head towards Oost to the *Hortus Botanicus* garden and have a wander through there. The *Dappermarkt* is real authentic Amsterdam along with Javastraat, an area you would once never go to, which now features some of my favourite shops. I would then take the ferry to the North/IJplein and get a table at *Hotel De Goudfazant*, they have been a great example for us. Then I would make my way back to the centre and have a drink at an old pub called *'t Loosje*, which I have been visiting for more than 30 years.

How would you like the future of food to evolve in the city?

The chefs of Amsterdam have been very conscious in working together as a community. We get together every year or so, drink, eat and discuss food. No press. No patrons. Just us enjoying each other's company. It means we can discuss concerns, or swap tips or offer advice. What I would really like to do is invite farmers into this community so that we can work more closely with their seasonal produce. They can give us what they can grow, and we design our menus around that.

Give us a food tip people would not expect from you…

I love a good Indonesian satay. But I really appreciate Surinamese food, especially the Indian-style Suriname kitchen that not many know about until they visit the Netherlands. My favourite is *De Hapjeshoek* just under Waterlooplein inside the metro station. Their salt cod sandwiches are €3 and worth every cent.

Above: Amsterdam's Hortus Botanicus is one of the oldest botanical gardens worldwide
Below: RIJKS: a fine dining institution with attitude from Joris Bijdendijk

Do Unto Others

Nick Schonfeld

When I moved from London to Amsterdam in 2003, I had no intention of staying. A quick in-and-out. A year or two at most. Sixteen years later and I still haven't left.

First, a little context: I am Dutch. Well, technically. I was born in The Hague, but mostly lived abroad until I was 23 years old. My mother, brother, sister and I moved from country to country, following my father who worked for a large conglomerate.

I grew up wherever the company sent us. Argentina, Portugal, the United States, Germany, Switzerland. Each time we'd settle in a new international school and make new friends. Then we, or they, would leave again. Everything was always changing. Nothing was forever. Nothing was normal. The only constants were diversity and tolerance.

In case you are not familiar with international schools, they're sheltered and privileged places, filled with the children of diplomats and CEOs. But they're also fascinating cultural melting pots where, no matter how foreign or strange or otherwise diverse you are, everybody gets along. There was no bullying or discrimination that I can remember. No us versus them. We were all different. That was our mutual deterrence. If I would have singled someone out because of their ethnicity or nationality, my own "difference" would immediately negate it. There would be no point.

By tolerating those around us we helped maintain a stable environment in which we would ourselves be tolerated. Obviously, we made friends the normal way (one of those friends I met 22 years ago in Hamburg, Germany for example, shares an office with me today), but most of my relationships were initially based on the very practical need to get along. Life was easier that way.

A friend of mine who works as a tour guide recently told me about an old Amsterdam saying: "Het maakt me niet uit als je op tafel sch**t, zolang het maar niet op mijn bord spettert". Roughly translated it means "I don't care if you sh*t on the table, as long as none of it gets on my plate." I apologise for this analogy's crudeness, but I feel it perfectly encapsulates the city's approach to tolerance. Do what you want, as long as it doesn't affect me. If you're 80 years old and you want to rollerblade through the city wearing only a thong, fine. I'll even lace up your boots. Just don't ask me to perform fishtails with you in the park.

What struck me in particular was not the defecating part of the statement, but the "... as long as none of it gets on my plate." There is a real libertarian streak to the people who live here, myself included. "Doe normaal" or "Be normal" is a good way to break the ice. As I write this, my downstairs neighbour is pumping rock music out of her stereo. My floor is vibrating. It's eleven o'clock on a Saturday night. If I complain too early, I risk her complaining right back when I crank up the volume, but if I complain too late, I will have set a dangerous precedent, one she is sure to abuse in the near future. I will wait until one in the morning, and if she hasn't turned it down by then, I'll go knock on her door. It's nuanced, I'll give you that, but if you live here long enough, you'll get the hang of it.

Amsterdam is famously pragmatic about its tolerance and has been for a thousand years, if not longer. The city's "gedoogbeleid" —the practice of not enforcing certain laws in favour of a tolerant approach, made famous by our coffeeshops and Red Light District— has been around in some form or other, for as long as anyone can remember. Over the centuries it has moved with the times, but the building blocks have remained the same: libertarianism, capitalism and socialism. So, when I say tolerance, I mean tolerate. There is a difference. In most cases, acceptance of others does not come from some abstract utopian place of togetherness. It comes from the very practical, self-serving need to make sure oneself is tolerated.

To wit, I work in a former shipyard called NDSM. Inside a vast hall artists and squatters built a maze of studios, small workshops and co-working spaces called Art City, and I rent one of these units. Although subsidised by the city, and overseen by a foundation, we are largely left to "govern" ourselves. The place is a controlled mess; the kind that is just dirty enough to look creative and raw, but not so filthy that it puts off the tourists.

Some Art City residents have been there since the beginning and regularly use the defecating-on-the-table analogy. Others, like me, are relative newcomers. But everyone accepts each other's quirks: the incessantly annoying whine of an angle-grinder, a twice-weekly terrible sounding band-practice, countless music video shoots. My outdoor toasty-grilling would surely be an issue. My insistence on parking my bike under the stairs would cause problems. My attempts at stopping tourists from clambering up the hall's iron girders for a death-defying selfie would be snubbed. These are things we tolerate because if we didn't, our lives would become impossible. The unique composition of Art City, metalworkers, perfumers, DJ's, designers, drum kit manufacturers and 3D printers would cease to exist.

Diversity and tolerance equal stability. But only to a point. Go too far in one direction, and things become unstable. This is the way they set up international schools. This is also Amsterdam's secret formula. Its very soul. The moment you tip the scales, it's over. Too much sameness and the wheels come off. After all, an international school with only a few nationalities is no longer international. And so, Amsterdam's gedoogbeleid has become my gedoogbeleid.

Amsterdam has an energy that is only possible thanks to this mixing and fusing of different cultures. The city is constantly changing. New stores, restaurants and bars are opening and closing at an astonishing rate. A Korean kimchi store, two new ramen places and a high-end Peruvian restaurant launched on my high-street in the last year. I think one of the ramen places has already closed. At school too, friends would come and go. Japanese replaced by French replaced by Iranian. It is something I remember experiencing as a child: an excited feeling whenever a teacher would announce a new student was joining the year. Where would they be from? Where is Bamako? Do they speak English in Taiwan?

When I walk down the street in my neighbourhood, I will hear French, German, Italian or English before Dutch. Around the corner from my apartment a Sardinian engineer who speaks three words of Dutch opened a fresh pasta shop (which he took over from an American woman who made red velvet cakes and peanut brittle.) Pass by my local yoga studio and you'll hear the instructor tell her students to stretch more in a thick New York accent.

A diverse group of nationalities and cultures living together in a small, compact environment; united by English as the common language; using their differences to include and not exclude; tolerating each other for the sake of stability. To me there are plenty of similarities between life in Amsterdam and life in an international school.

It is why, after 16 years, I still haven't left. Yes, it is beautiful, especially in summer. Yes, it's great that the city is both a village and a metropolis. Yes, the pace of life is just the right side of leisurely. But above all, Amsterdam reminds me of my childhood. Of being surrounded by people as different to me as I was to them. I love living here. I know it is a self-serving, pragmatic love, but I don't care.

Nick Schonfeld is a writer based in Amsterdam. After an existential revelation he quit his job in advertising and began splitting his time between writing screenplays and children's books and raising awareness for social and environmental issues including a fund in Malawi that focuses on youth employability. Originally published in 2019.

Titia van Beckum, DJ

Rewind

Titia van Beckum
One of the promising emerging artists in Amsterdam's music scene, Titia van Beckum aka Titia began spinning for fun at parties as part of the Supergirls DJ collective. Quickly rising through the ranks, her busy schedule now includes Europe's most storied electronic music venues and festivals

Master of the eclectic set—where house, acid and techno converge—Titia has been taking over the electronic music world since her Boiler Room debut. But before all that, she has divulged her Amsterdam favourites, from late night eats to well-stocked record shops

Shelter
Noord

Warehouse Elementenstraat
Westpoort

Garage Noord
Noord

Distortion Records
Centrum

Bordello A Parigi
Centrum

Killacutz
Centrum

FC Hyena
Noord

Skatecafe
Noord

Het Smikkelhoekje
Noord

Hotel de Goudfazant
Noord

Coba
Noord

Klaproos
Noord

Oedipus Brewing
Noord

How did living in Amsterdam play a role in you becoming a breakthrough artist in the DJ scene?

I started DJing in Eindhoven, the city I grew up in. It's a nice city with occasionally great underground initiatives, but there were no real clubs or regular raves there. I mostly played at the bar where me and my friends from the Design Academy hung out all the time. When I moved to Amsterdam all of a sudden there were so many venues and events to play. It made a huge difference.

What are the important venues in Amsterdam's nightlife scene?

I'd say *Shelter*, *Warehouse Elementenstraat*, and *Garage Noord*.

Any other local DJs who you've been following lately?

There are many local DJs, many good ones. More and more female DJs as well who are doing really great things. Everyone has their own style of music which I really like. But if there's one to name I would say Súya. He happens to be a good friend of mine; we share the same thoughts when it comes to music. He has a great collection and taste in music. There are not many DJs who can really surprise me with sick records like he does.

Where do you go after a long night out to get some wholesome food?

Oh wholesome is a tricky one. Maybe you should go home and eat a banana. I try to avoid late night dining, but sometimes when I really can't resist the need I go to that döner place on the corner of the back of Central Station, at the ferry side, and order a Pita Halloumi. It's really good.

How do you spend your time off in Amsterdam when you're not busy with festivals and gigs?

When I'm not working at the Clone Records store in Rotterdam or making music, I love being with my girlfriend or hanging out with friends. I like going to a museum, or lately I like to take a walk. I like having lunches, brunches or dinners with wine! I live in the north and like this area a lot. Sometimes I play soccer. I daydream a lot. And sometimes I draw stuff.

Any favourite record shops in Amsterdam?

I would say *Distortion Records*. That place is a must-visit. You almost can't walk inside the shop because of all the cardboard boxes and records everywhere, but the owner knows where to find that particular record you just asked for, in two seconds. I also really like *Bordello A Parigi*, they have a good selection, and *Killacutz* sometimes has some good secondhand stuff.

What are some major raves and festivals in the Netherlands that dance music fans should not miss?

Of course, you have the IsBurning parties, Dekmantel Festival, and you have parties organized by ZeeZout and Cartel. I also really liked Wildeburg.

Any other Amsterdam favourites?

100% the North! For a walk along the IJ, *FC Hyena* for cinema and wine, *Skatecafe* and *Garage Noord* for drinks and clubbing, snack bar *Het Smikkelhoekje* for simply the best place in town, dinner at *Hotel de Goudfazant* or *Coba*, the pizza place *Klaproos*, *Oedipus Taproom*, I could go on and on.

Walk on the Wild Side

A showcase by Isabella Rozendaal

The private fauna of Dutch capital residents is the subject of "Animalia," commissioned by the Amsterdam City Archives. The city's pets are just as much a part of Amsterdam's history as its people, says Rozendaal, who has photographed 110 animals to date

Isabella Rozendaal & Michiel Schuurman
Isabella is a photographer whose latest project, "Animalia", has taken her to all corners of Amsterdam. Her husband, Michiel, started off as a graffiti artist before becoming one of the city's most innovative graphic and textile designers

Isabella Rozendaal & Michiel Schuurman,
Photographer & Graphic Designer

Staying Put

Her work takes her all over the world. His designs are world-renowned. Yet this creative power couple can't imagine living anywhere other than Amsterdam. Isabella and Michiel talk to us about their love of all things Oost and why the city holds them captive

Vlieger
Centrum

Athenaeum Boekhandel
Centrum

The American Book Center
Centrum

Waterstones
Centrum

TonTon Club
West

How did you two meet?

Isabella: Through working together. Michiel designed my second photography book, which was about Dutch people on vacation.

Michiel: Isabella's brother was an old classmate of mine, and she came to my studio looking for a graphic designer. Two books later we got married.

Tell us a bit about your neighbourhood.

Isabella: We live in Oost, the eastern part of the city. Initially, we got this apartment because of its unusual layout, but now we very much enjoy living here. The area has changed a lot since we moved in, although it's become gentrified like so many places in Amsterdam, it's also kept a lot of its original character.

Michiel: I was born in Oost and I went to school here so I knew the neighbourhood well. I've never lived in any other city. It surprises people when they hear I've only ever lived in Amsterdam.

It's rare to find someone who has lived in Amsterdam their entire life. What is it about the city that keeps you here?

Michiel: I love our neighbourhood. I love walking out of our apartment and into an area that feels real, a great mix of cultures and income levels. Oost is such a diverse place. I just never left. There is a real cohesion to this city. People really live together.

Isabella: Also, by now we have established strong professional networks here. We're both freelancers and although I frequently travel for work, most of our commissions originate in Amsterdam. So, the city is a great base for us.

Michiel: For me, Amsterdam is like an old leather jacket, a super comfortable fit. I know every street in the city; all of its folds and creases and scratches. It's very familiar.

Tell me about your ideal day off in Amsterdam.

Isabella: I enjoy going around to my favourite stores. *Vlieger*, a 150-year-old paper shop where you can buy every kind of paper imaginable.

Michiel: It's a place where mothers and professionals go to buy their art supplies.

Isabella: I'm a big fan of bookstores, so places like *Athenaeum Boekhandel*, *The American Book Center* or *Waterstones* are the perfect day-off location for me.

Michiel: I like to walk through *Athenaeum Boekhandel*. I'll take a random tram to the last stop on the line and then walk back home. It's a great way to stay in touch with the city.

Isabella: We also love to eat and to cook.

Michiel: Yes. We do a lot of cooking when we have the time.

Isabella: We visit the organic market on the Nieuwmarkt every Saturday. That's where I buy all my vegetables for the week.

Michiel: And if you are a pinball addict like me, then make sure you go to the *TonTon Club*, a great retro arcade and board game bar.

Isabella, you've photographed lots of Amsterdam animals for your project "Animalia". Any memorable stories?

Isabella: I remember one lady in particular. She lived in a tiny house with sixteen miniature dachshunds. That was a full house I can tell you. Another time, I spent a very emotional afternoon with a woman and the cremated remains of her dead horse. What's special about this project is that it gives me access to places and people that I would normally never get to see or meet.

Ground from scratch: Hartog's Wholegrain Bakery is famed not just for bread but for sweets like apple buns

Sea Palace
Centrum

Hartog's Volkoren
Oost

Isabella, you are a bit of a foodie. What are some of your favourite place to eat out?

Isabella: I'm mainly interested in places that don't feel like restaurants. So, no fine dining. I like to get a sense of the soul and personality behind the food. I want to feel relaxed when I eat. Dim sum at the *Sea Palace* is great. It looks like a real tourist trap, but the food is beyond good. And hands-down the best bakery is *Hartog's Volkoren* on the Wibautstraat. They grind their own flour, it's all wholegrain and delicious.

Michiel, tell us about your beginnings in art.

Michiel: I started off as a graffiti artist and a skater, from age twelve until my thirties. I had no idea that graffiti would lead to a career in art. Unlike with Isabella, whose father and brother are both artists, there are no artists in my family. So, it took me a long time to figure out that my tagging could become something more substantial.

Has your graffiti background influenced your work?

Michiel: You can definitely see it now. For a while, I wanted to get away from it and explore unrelated styles, but it slowly seeped back into my work. My colour knowledge, what techniques work well, that kind of thing. Skateboarding too is still an influence. I'm too old for it now, but the drive I had then—to overcome obstacles and pain to become the best—that's something I still use today.

Rijksmuseum
Zuid

Stedelijk Museum
Zuid

Foam
Centre

Huis Marseille
Centrum

Eye Filmmuseum
Noord

Upstream Gallery
Centrum

You are known for bold, striking and complex works. What is it about Amsterdam that inspires you?

Michiel: I use colour, specifically fluorescent colours to create work that is different from many of my peers. There is a strong tendency to create black and white work at the moment, which I don't find interesting. Similarly, Amsterdam stands out from the rest of the Netherlands. It's far more colourful and layered than many other cities.

Michiel, your work is part of the Stedelijk Museum Collection. What other museums or galleries do you think are worth visiting?

Michiel: I'm afraid it's the usual suspects: *Rijksmuseum*, *Stedelijk Museum*, *Foam*.

Isabella: *Huis Marseille* and the *Eye Filmmuseum* have great exhibitions too, which few people know. *Upstream Gallery* is great too. But I am biased because they represent my brother, Rafaël Rozendaal.

You collaborate with other artists and designers...

Michiel: I'm proud of having worked with Boris Tellegen aka Delta, one of my graffiti heroes. I'm working on a series of bags together with a great fashion designer called Susan Bijl. Also, I work together with Vlisco, a Dutch textile company. I worked for them for four years and you can still find a lot of my textile designs there.

Isabella: And you can find the fakes of those fabrics on Albert Cuyp market.

Michiel: That's true. It's actually a thing I enjoy. Finding and buying fake versions of my own designs. It's the ultimate compliment.

There is one very special collaboration you did with Isabella. Can you tell us more about that?

Michiel: I designed Isabella's wedding dress. That was very special. Super nerve-wracking, but special.

Isabella: I had recently visited Brazil and wanted a colourful dress; something that reflected the amazing colour palette you find there. Michiel is the master of colour so I asked him to make it.

Michiel: What was interesting is that I ended up using several techniques I had never used before, to get the colours to blend the way they do. I didn't know if it would work.

Isabella: My favourite moment was when he saw the dress for the first time on our wedding day. His face was priceless. He looked so relieved.

Michiel: I had seen the printed fabric, but once the dressmaker took over, I saw nothing of it until the day of our wedding.

Isabella and Michiel, you both have very different but equally fascinating relationships with the city. Can you imagine ever living anywhere else?

Isabella: A definitive no.

Michiel: No. Never. I mean we've talked about it, but no. I can imagine living somewhere else in Oost, but it will always be Amsterdam.

Isabella: Even though my experience of the city is so different from that of Michiel, I think we both really call this place home. There are so many fragments of identity that come together here.

Upstream Gallery presented "Northstar", the first solo exhibition of Tabor Robak in the Netherlands

Centrum

Beyond the Bridges

Between the Red Light stag party route and coffee shops are a maze of concept stores, vintage troves and organic eateries offering a different view on the Amsterdam city centre

Shop Let the Music Play

With one of the most vibrant vinyl scenes in the world, you need just scratch Amsterdam's surface to find record troves and a rich vein of parties. In the murky depths of the Red Light District, record store and label *Bordello A Parigi* (pictured) is a headquarter for obscure electronic music, Italo and disco with merchandise you'll want to buy in bulk. Also in walking distance: *Vintage Voudou, Record Friend,* and *Rush Hour*. If music is your medicine, drop by *Red Light Radio,* and check live broadcasts of touring DJs, local aficionados and party people spinning discs between the windows of working girls. Chill your rock boots at the oldest record store in the city *Concerto,* situated along hip shopping street Utrechtsestraat. It offers indie, rock and alternative vibes of every kind. With in-store acoustic sessions and last-minute concert tickets on offer, take it as your plug socket into the city's sonic mainframe.

• Various locations, Centrum

Night Pull Up a Stool

An old man's bar in the true sense of the term, this corner pub with no website, no cash register, no card acceptance and no English-speaking staff is one of the best the Centre has to offer. Bring cash. Be ready to play a board game. Be on board to accept raw meats, cheese and mustard offered up on a plank while you sip on red wine or ales. Just don't expect to be treated like anything other than a local at *Café de Wetering*. A wood fire in winter and streetside drinking in summer makes this a personality pub for all seasons.
• Café de Wetering, Weteringstraat 37

Shop True Cost

Designers used to float into Amsterdam in pursuit of inspiration, but the flood has dried up as vintage stores dwindled in number and quality. For the real thing without markup or upcycling of chain thrift shop wares, *Bis!*, *Tamago*—and especially *Concrete Matter* with its selection of rare Americana (pictured)—are old-world secondhand stores whose people have a keen eye for a silhouette and designer clothing with a story.
• Various locations, Centrum

Food Parisdam

An institution bringing the Parisian bistronomie take to the Dutch capital is to be found among the city chaos at *Kaagman en Kortekaas*. Based in a former Russian salon, the duo behind it fill it with the smells and flavours of farm-fresh food, with much game and poultry accompanied by well-sourced wines. They tend to make their own charcuterie and terrines, leaving not much for the vegetarians, so be warned. Dressed in chambray, wait staff serve with that "gezellig"—or typical Dutch cosy—vibe.
• Kaagman en Kortekaas, Sint Nicolaasstraat 43, kaagmanenkortekaas.nl

Night — Sedimentary

Named after the French slang term for to drink profusely, *Glouglou* is a buzzy corner bar with a bottle shop attached. For punters unafraid of a little sediment, this spot has been serving preservative-free organic wines since before they turned widespread. Bar snacks are simple, people are in abundance and old-fashioned service will have you staying here for way more than a "couple of glasses."

• Glouglou, Tweede van der Helststraat 3, glouglou.nl

Shop — Street to Catwalk

Urban explorers can investigate the upscale side of streetwear at *Concrete*. Hand-picked items from limited editions and collaborations include mainstay brands like Adidas Originals, Asics, Diodora and The North Face as well as high-end fashion from Marni or Walter Van Beirendonck. *Maha Amsterdam* points in the same direction but for female streetwear enthusiasts. The brand opened in 2015 with its own apparel line, featuring relaxed staples designed with women in mind. It's evolved into a multi-brand store that offers a curated selection of sneakers and fashion items. If you need a quick break, grab a coffee or cookie next door at *Cafe Maha Amsterdam*.

• Various locations, Centrum

Shop — Tread Softly

What started as sneaky trips overseas to gather kicks for friends became one of the leading sneaker stores. Patta has been supplying Amsterdam skateboarders, DJs and kids with limited-edition Vans, Nikes and Adidas. With their base in Chinatown's Zeedijk—one of the oldest streets in Amsterdam—they've formed a posse of underground stores hidden among Sichuan restaurants, a Buddhist temple and costume shops. Along with *The New Originals*, a fashion brand designed for creatives and rooted in the city's art, music and nightlife scenes, this busy street will pack your bags.

• Various locations, Centrum

Shop Dedicated Design

Stylish, somewhat affordable, and an institution, *droog* (pictured) is a rabbit hole of discoveries just outside the Red Light District. There's accommodation in the One and Only Bedroom situated in the roof, events at the space Hôtel Droog, high tea and good coffee at Cafe-droog and the Fairy Tale Garden offers a glimpse into gardening done the droog way. An essential store of Dutch design, this spot has been supplying the world with collaborations, concepts and anti-disciplinary design since 1993. Forget tulip bulbs or Amsterdam beanies, a real souvenir might be a red-roofed birdfeeder or a tablecloth "stained" with the aftermath of a dinner party. Local avant garde is represented here via designers from Marcel Wanders to unknown upcoming talents. While there, hop across the canal for *DSIGN*—a retail chain described as "candy stores" for Dutch design enthusiasts—to pick up a Lexon Mina lamp, a 2D felt bag or other boutique accessories.

• Various locations, Centrum

Jelani Isaacs
He lived in Berlin, Barcelona and New York before setting up shop in the Netherlands. His venture New Amsterdam is a hybrid between production company and advertising agency. As chief executive producer, Jelani takes care of the film side

Jelani Isaacs, Producer

City Buff

Isaacs has experienced Amsterdam in ways that most of us never will. From rescuing Eminem to the best electric skateboards and his porterhouse steak of choice, this seasoned producer and self-professed sneaker-addict recounts his canal-side stories

Pathé Tuschinski
Centrum

Pathé De Munt
Centrum

The Movies
Centrum

Patta
Centre

Nyonya
Centrum

Café Jakarta
Oost

Choux
Centrum

Rijsel
Oost

You based your company in Amsterdam. What makes this city unique?

It's just such vibrant, culturally enhanced, art loving and inclusive place. Amsterdam embraces many forms of self-expression and creativity. For example, the building that houses our office is a "facade church." From the outside it looks like a normal canal house but inside they used it as a place of worship for Christians, Jews and Muslims alike. Everyone can be themselves here, yet we are able to live together in a compact city.

Where do you live and why?

In the city's east, in Zeeburg, which I think is the most vibrant of the six boroughs. I live on the top floor of an apartment building and my windows are so thick that it's wonderfully quiet. But, as soon as I take one step outside, I'm in the middle of town, and everybody and everything is on the move.

You've filmed a lot of commercials and movies in Amsterdam. What are some of your favourite locations?

The Reguliersgracht, with its seven bridges is amazing, especially at night. The Brouwersgracht, as well. Both are beautiful examples of traditional Amsterdam architecture and city living. The people who live there are very down to earth, with a real sense of community.

Any behind-the-scenes stories you can share with us?

Wow. Too many to mention. While we were shooting in the Red Light District, myself and a group of local pimps had to rescue Eminem from a bunch of drunken English tourists. Also, I once did a Bollywood movie, "When Harry Met Sejal," with Shah Rukh Khan. I had gotten approval for a night shoot from the city council, but word had gotten out that Shah Rukh would be there. There must have been like 20,000 fans screaming his name at one in the morning. The only way to get them to stop was the man himself asking them to be quiet. Imagine. Thousands upon thousands of people standing quietly, for seven hours.

You travel a lot. What do you miss most while you're gone?

The city's village feel. I can go from the office, to lunch on a terrace, to a playground with my kids, to a burger place for dinner, and all of it is within walking distance. Everything is so much more accessible compared to other capital cities. I think that's what attracts so many expats to Amsterdam. That, and how unconcerned people are here with celebrities. You'd be surprised how many famous actors and musicians have a discreet pied-à-terre here. They feel they can be themselves and that people will leave them alone. Unless you're Shah Rukh Khan.

What do you do when you're not working?

I'm a big movie buff, so I spend a lot of my downtime in cinemas like *Pathé Tuschinski* or *De Munt*. But also in smaller theatres like *The Movies*. Other than that, I have a serious sneaker addiction so I often go to *Patta* on the Zeedijk. They have a unique collection of tier zero shoes. I'm also a bit of a foodie. Thanks to Amsterdam's diversity, we have a high concentration of good quality restaurants here. You might have to search them out, but that is half the fun for me. Amazing Thai food, Malaysian restaurants like *Nyonya*, Indonesian restaurants like *Café Jakarta*.

Rijsel: Famous for the chicken and its laid back atmosphere

BAK
Centrum

A-Fusion
Centrum

Café Bern
Centrum

Hiding In Plain Sight
Centrum

Cafe Stevens
Centrum

Bar Bukowski
Oost

Mr Porter
Centrum

In that case, let's imagine some hungry clients just arrived from Los Angeles. Where do you take them?

Well, flights from LA land in the morning, but they'll be on evening time so probably *Choux*, exquisite food, chic and delicious. Or *Rijsel* for their legendary chicken. Or *BAK* for the view. Or *A-Fusion* for the sushi, or *Café Bern* for the cheese fondue. Ha! I guess it depends on what they feel like eating.

It sounds like your clients will be well fed. But what if they want a drink instead?

Go for cocktails at *Hiding In Plain Sight*. Or *Cafe Stevens* on the Nieuwmarkt if they want to experience a typical Dutch bar.

Any traditional Dutch culinary highlights you can recommend?

A kroket from a FEBO, a kind of giant walk-in vending machine, which you can find all over the city. For raw herring with onions and pickles, try the third stall at the Albert Cuyp Market. Oh, and mixed fried snacks at *Bar Bukowski*.

You are a self-professed carnivore. So… porterhouse or ribeye?

I would always say porterhouse.

And where do you find the best one?

Mr Porter on top of the W Hotel on the Spuistraat. It's a crazy place with a rooftop pool, but the meat is superb there.

Dutch Touch

The Family

• Louis Andriessen, Ruud Bos Orchestra, 1973

A standout light of Dutch classical avant-garde music, Andriessen's decades-long career has seen his rebellious touch caress pieces from political performance to stage plays. This film soundtrack for director Lodewijk de Boer is a detour into the pop-jazz side of his genius.

Books

Dammed
• L. G. Rivera, 2011

A trip to Amsterdam leads two work companions into a whole new world of discovery: the hidden pleasures of the city and the fragility of mental sanity. "Dammed" fills the reader's imagination with exalting experiences and a subtle downward spiral into the darkness of one's own mind.

Amsterdam!
• Ed van Der Elsken, 1979

Ed van Der Elsken has perfectly captured the everyday lifestyle of post-war Amsterdam. The iconic Dutch lensman's street photography gives us a beautiful glimpse of the capital through the faces of its inhabitants over the decades.

Outsider in Amsterdam
• Janwillem Van De Wetering, 1975

A murder mystery set in the streets of Amsterdam sheds light on a newly developed religious commune. This gripping novel manages to transcend the moral dilemmas of the open drug culture of the city in the 1970s.

Movies

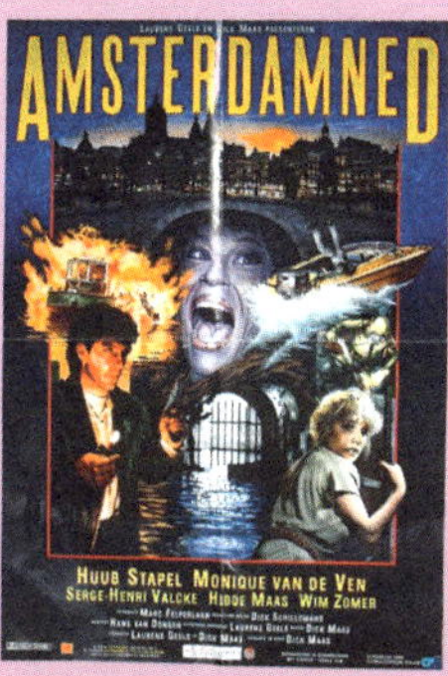

Amsterdamned
• Dick Maas, 1988

Blood, thrills, explosions. This typical 1980s action film lets you explore the streets and canals of the Dutch capital by way of a cliffhanging serial murder investigation. An intense speedboat chase serves up an in-depth tour of the city.

Turkish Delight
• Paul Verhoeven, 1973

A sex scene in the rain and Rutger Hauer riding a bicycle through the streets of Amsterdam—what could be more Dutch? Based on a novel by Jan Wolkers, this film has become a Dutch classic, portraying the era of sexual liberation in the capital.

Borgman
• Alex van Warmerdam, 2013

A luxurious residential area just outside of Amsterdam provides the perfect juxtaposition for this absurd story. Watch the psychological games unfold in this wonderfully twisted tale.

Music

My Way
• Herman Brood, 2001

The Dutch enfant terrible's last album is arguably his best. Released posthumously, it mixes sounds from a range of rock and blues greats, from Chet Baker to Sid Vicious. In his interpretations you can hear the strain in his voice, only intensified by his drug habit at the time, which eventually led to his suicide in 2001.

The Kyteman Orchestra
• The Kyteman Orchestra, 2012

Okay, the brain behind The Orchestra, Colin Benders, is not from Amsterdam, but Utrecht. But he and the other 18 musicians, singers and choir members create an utterly unique experience, not to be missed. Lose yourself in this otherworldly blend of soul, hip-hop, pop and classical music.

Cabinet Of Curiosities
• Jacco Gardner, 2013

This young man from Hoorn, just north of Amsterdam, keeps the hippie spirit alive. With his music he digs deep into the heritage of the 1960s psychedelica sound.

STUNTMAN
MICK JOHAN

Stuntman

Mick Johan

I used to live above a Turkish bakery on the east side of Amsterdam. The owner of the bakery was a man named Mustafa, a solid man, bald and of stocky build. He also owned a Turkish coffeehouse across the street, a dark place with a shady aura. I never set foot inside. Mustafa spent most of his days smoking cigarettes while shaking other men's hands in front of the establishment. Shaking hands appeared to be a main activity of his work. Whenever we met Mustafa would shake my hand as well. He was good at it. His hands were soft and hairy, the thick flesh on his fingers was slowly overgrowing his unsubtle golden rings.

"You good?" He would ask, and I would nod. A firm grip between two men. I took pride in this relationship. This tiny daily ritual between two grown male human beings of which one (spoiler alert: me) was still very much a boy, made me feel like I was part of something big and tribal that I understood nothing of. A handshake like a gateway to a hidden world in our neighbourhood, invisible to my eyes.

Every night around 4am the nightshift opened the bakery door to cool off the first batch of baked croissants. Coming home after a night out was bliss; the smell of fresh baked pastry would guide me home and the guys working would always let me buy something even if the shop was still closed. One night I came home and found a tall slender guy I never saw before smoking outside the bakery. He was wearing the red baker's apron and leaned against the doorpost. It was a cold night and the steaming heat that came out of the shop seemed to come right from him. A man on fire. As I approached the smell of fresh baked goods blended perfectly with the sweet smell of cigarette smoke. I sensed him watching me as I was locking my bike, which took me a while since I was mildly intoxicated, but instead of creepy or threatening, it was kind of soothing. As I finally got up from the hassle that was my bicycle lock, I looked him in the eyes. He took a massive drag of his cigarette, spread his arms and yelled out: "Welcome home. Did you have a good night, my friend? You're drunk, aren't you?"

"Maybe." I said, not sure if I was.

"Come and sit with me for a bit."

He conjured up a chair from out of nowhere, sat me down and gave me a smoke. "You are our neighbour, it's nice to meet you." He lit up my cigarette.

"Nice to meet you too." I mumbled, almost losing my smoke. "Do you work here?"

He laughed at me.

"You really are drunk."

I shrugged apologetically.

"What's your name?" I asked.

He threw away his cigarette, walked back to the middle of the sidewalk and spread his arms, while drawing a wide circle around his left foot

Illustration: Jonathan Niclaus

with his right foot. He raised his arms until the back of his hands touched each other. He was a toreador? The cigarette tasted like black market.

"I ... am ... stuntman Hawar!" He looked like a villain introducing himself in a sixties superhero movie. He took a bow, reaching out his hand towards me. I shook it. He had beautiful long fingers.

"My name is Frido, and I'm drunk."

"Frido? What are you, a hobbit?" He laughed.

"No, no. I mean, yeah, but no." I wished I never took this awful tasting cigarette.

"Well Hobbit, I am Hawar. Stuntman Hawar. I'm from Kurdistan, I live in the Netherlands for three months now. Are you on Facebook? Let's be friends."

"Sure." I said as he finally released my hand.

"Where's your phone? Let's be friends. Give me your phone."

I took out my phone and opened the app. I wanted to tell him I was never on Facebook anymore, but I didn't and I gave him my phone.

"So, eh, do you like Amsterdam?" For a brief moment I could hear what Uber drivers heard when I was in their cars trying to make conversation.

"Check this out." He showed me his Facebook profile picture. He was sitting on a motorcycle wearing a colourful leather suit with flames on it. It matched the flames on the bike. The sky was grey and although there were some grassy hills in the back it felt like they were somewhere in a desert. A bunch of kids surrounded him, looking at the camera as if they had met Jesus himself. One of them was wearing his helmet. He wore a great pair of shades and a cigarette was dangling in the corner of his mouth. He looked like a superstar.

"Great photo." I said, and it was.

I felt bad about being drunk. I had always wanted to befriend a refugee, but not when I was drunk. I wondered if I should give him some clothes. My face turned red and I quickly pushed the 'send friend request' button.

"Wait, let me show you some action." He grabbed the phone out of my hand again.

"Look." He showed me a movie of a biker riding a wall of death. His arms were spread. The speed was insane. It was like a cartoon of wild animal raging in a cage. I recognised the suit, it was him. His cape was fluttering behind him. The movie cut to a new scene at the Wall of Death. Hawar was now holding a baby on his bike while rapidly going in vertical circles. The crowd was raging now. It was out of this world.

"Do you hear them? The crowd? Do you know what Hawar means?" He left me no time to answer. "It means scream. My name means scream in Sorani."

He gave me back my phone.

"I never met a stuntman before."

"I used to do jumps too. I lived around Erbil, in Iraqi Kurdistan. They called me Erbil Knievel sometimes." He grinned.

"Like Evil Knievel." I said, quite unnecessary.

"Yeah, minus the satanic reference because people are very religious around Erbil." He grabbed a croissant from the bakery.

"Why did you come to Amsterdam? I mean, you're a stuntman. That's a dream." He lit up a new cigarette and gave me the croissant.

As I ate, there was a silence. I could hear the cigarette crackle gently in the thin early winter air. The croissant was salty and greasy, but exactly what I needed.

"How old are you?"

"27." I answered.

"Perfect age to die." He smiled.

"I know." Part of me wanted to die, but it was the same part that had all the plans and never came through.

"I'm 33. Same age as Jesus when he died. Being dead is easier than being alive." He looked up and took another drag of his cigarette.

"Do you have a family?" I shook my head. I didn't even have a girlfriend. I had parents, and some plants, but they were all dying. The plants, not my parents.

"I have a son and a wife. They still live close to Erbil." He paused to give me a chance to ask for their names or pictures, but I didn't.

He grinned: "ISIS doesn't like stunts. We had to flee. Mustafa is a friend of my wife's family and he got me this job and a house, so I can send money to my family."

I fell completely silent, which made me feel stupid because I felt I had to say something. Then, way too late, something came: "Do you miss them?" I wanted to punch myself in the face.

"Who?"

"Well, your wife and child."

"Nopes." He chuckles at my baffled face.

"Wha... What do you mean?"

"I'm a stuntman, not a family man. They depend on me to send them money, and that's what I do."

"But what about your son?"

"What about him? He's five, he asks stupid questions and reeks of piss."

All of a sudden a woman was screaming angrily at the end of the street. She passed by us on her bicycle really fast, psychotically cursing. We watched her disappear in silence. Across the street the door of Mustafa's café opened and some men came out to see what was going on. They lit up a smoke and looked at us. Hawar looked at them, took a last drag of his cigarette and shot it into the street. "Responsibility is a nice distraction for the shortcomings of life." He smiled grimly.

"I gotta get back to work. Go to sleep, my friend. I'll see you around." Hawar patted me on the shoulder and went back inside the bakery.

He never accepted my friend request.

The first editor-in-chief of "Vice" in the Netherlands, Mick Johan is a writer, artist and drummer with the band MICH. His debut novel, "Totem Animal Arafat," was published in 2017.

006
v. Hameren Verhuur bv

LOST iN Partner Hotel

Pension Homeland

An affordable, retro-style hotel situated on a former historic naval base affords a green globe of harmonic peace just ten minutes from the lunacy of Amsterdam Central Station. Inside, the authentic continental sixties-style décor will transport you to the era in which the building was originally constructed—but without its former military occupants. Though you can still feel the vibe of the officers relaxing at the bar based in the former naval longroom. The range of drinks includes home-brewed products from the Pension Homeland-owned brewery just next door. And when it comes to dining, the restaurant offers homemade and seasonal cuisine—to be enjoyed in winter by a cosy fireplace, and in summer on the gorgeous terrace—following by a dip in the harbor swimming pool.

Pension Homeland, Kattenburgerstraat 5, Building 6, Amsterdam, pensionhomeland.com

Available from LOST iN

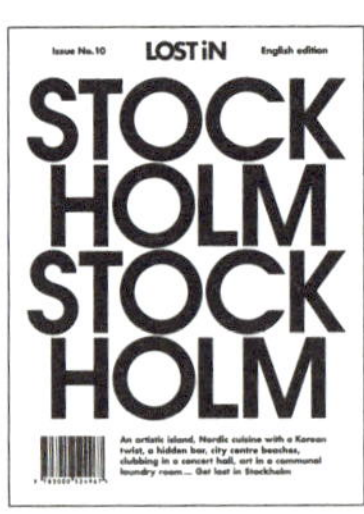

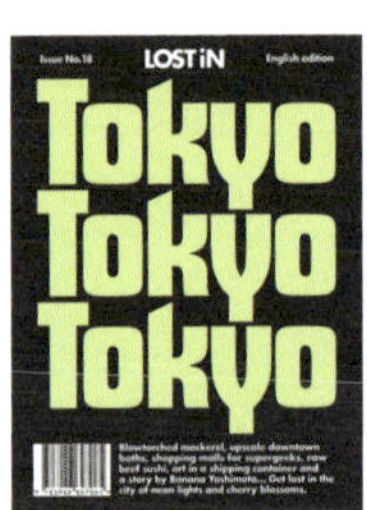

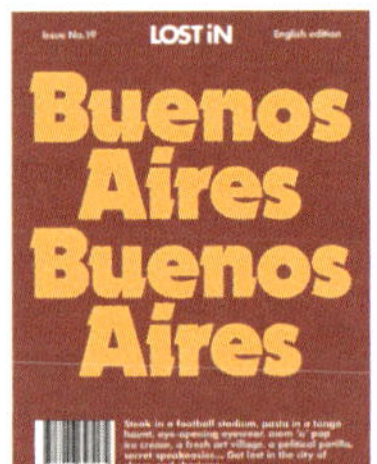

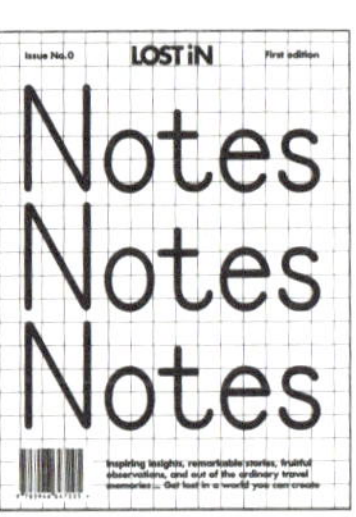

LOSTIN.COM